WWI
TRENCH FIGHTING
OF WORLD WAR I

JOHN HAMILTON

VISIT US AT

WWW.ABDOPUB.COM

Published by ABDO & Daughters, an imprint of ABDO Publishing Company, 4940 Viking Drive, Suite 622, Edina, Minnesota 55435. Copyright ©2004 by Abdo Consulting Group, Inc. International copyrights reserved in all countries. No part of this book may be reproduced in any form without written permission from the publisher.

Printed in the United States.

Edited by Jessica Klein
Graphic Design: John Hamilton
Cover Design: Mighty Media
Photos and illustrations:
    AP/Wide World Photo: 4, 17, 20, 27
    Corbis, p. 1, 6, 8, 9, 10, 12, 13, 15, 16, 19, 23, 24, 25,
    National Archives, p. 5, 14, 16, 21, 26, 32
    Photos of the Great War, p. 16, 18
    Cover photo: Corbis

Library of Congress Cataloging-in-Publication Data

Hamilton, John, 1959-
    Trench fighting of World War I / John Hamilton.
    p. cm.—(World War I)
    Includes index.
    Summary: An overview of trench warfare during World War I.
    ISBN 1-57765-916-3
    1. World War, 1914-1918—Trench warfare—Juvenile literature. 2. World War, 1914-1918—Campaigns—Western Front—Juvenile literature. [1. World War, 1914-1918—Trench warfare. 2. World War, 1914-1918—Campaigns—Western Front.] I. Title.

D530. H36 2003
940.4'1—dc21

               2002033296

TABLE OF CONTENTS

INTRODUCTION

And clink of shovels deepening the shallow trench.
The place was rotten with dead; green clumsy legs
High-booted, sprawled and grovelled along the saps
And trunks, face downward, in the sucking mud.
    —Siegfried Sassoon, Excerpt from "Counter-Attack"

Far right: A wounded soldier receives first aid in a trench at the Western Front.
Below: An American soldier throws a hand grenade at the enemy.

WORLD WAR I WAS THE FIRST major war to use what we think of today as modern weapons, such as machine guns and artillery. Many of the war's generals, however, were trained to fight grand, sweeping battles where cavalry charges, swords, and raw courage could win the day. It took them too long to fully realize how modern weapons changed warfare, and this resulted in tragic losses of human life.

Even before it started, WWI was called the Great War. It was supposed to be a grand spectacle; most people thought it would be finished quickly, fought on open terrain by huge armies pitting their wits and courage against each other. In August 1914, the German army invaded Belgium, and then swept through northeastern France. Many thought the French army was finished. The predictions of a quick war seemed to be coming true.

But by September 1914, the German army's push through France was stopped cold at the First Battle of the Marne. With their exhausted forces spread too thin, the Germans were forced to retreat.

After falling back and collecting reinforcements and supplies, the German army stopped. General Erich von Falkenhayn didn't want to give up any more captured French territory. He ordered his men to dig in and stop the Allied counterattacks. His troops dug shallow trenches in the ground and struck French and British troops with deadly blasts of machine guns and rifles.

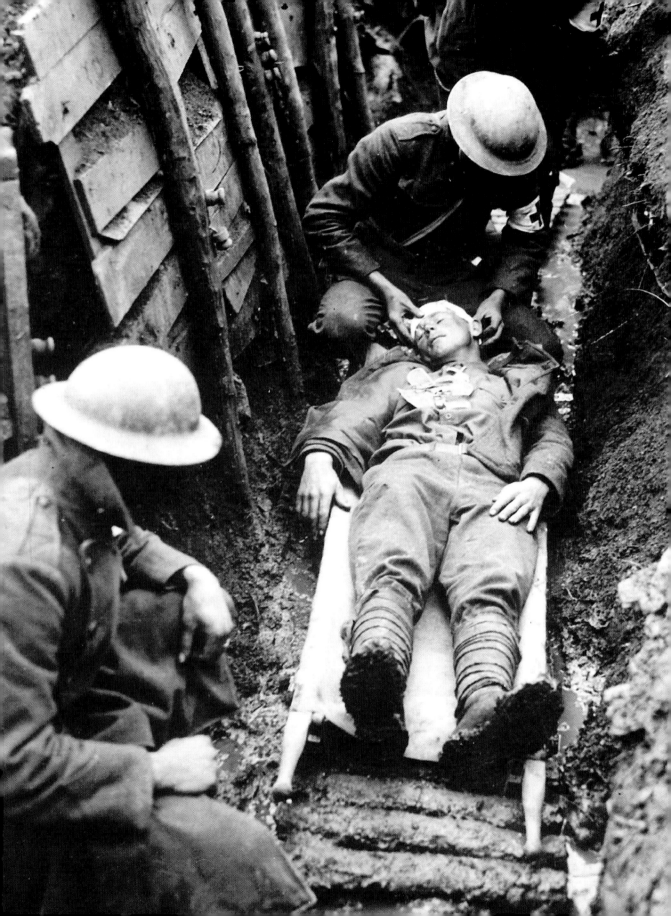

Above: During the first months of the war, trenches were simple ditches that gave only partial protection against enemy fire.

The Allies couldn't break through the German defenses, so they dug trenches of their own to protect themselves. All along the field of battle, defensive works were constructed. At first the trenches were nothing more than shallow ditches, but they eventually grew into elaborate systems of earthworks that shielded the men from the enemy. By the end of 1914, the trenches stretched from the North Sea all the way to the border of Switzerland. This line became the Western Front of World War I.

For many soldiers, leaving the trenches to charge the enemy meant almost certain death, or at the very least, horrible injury. But staying in the trenches was also a nightmare. Artillery, snipers, and poison gas killed thousands of soldiers even in the "safety" of the trenches. Most of these casualties never even saw the enemy; faceless death struck at them, seemingly at random, from out of nowhere.

If the enemy didn't strike down a soldier, living conditions soon did. Trenches were horrible places in which to live. They were filthy, infested with rodents and insects, and had few comforts such as toilets and running water. In the winter the trenches were frozen. In the summer, they were often wet and muddy.

Until the spring of 1918, the fighting in France was at a deadlock. The war of movement had become a stalemate. Nobody could figure out how to break through the enemy's defenses. Millions died trying. All sides continued launching disastrous frontal assaults against machine guns, rifles, and artillery, usually with little or no territory to show for the loss of life.

A French infantry officer, Alfred Joubaire, wrote in his diary before he was killed, "Humanity is mad! It must be mad to do what it is doing. What a massacre!" What was life like for the millions of men trapped in the trenches of World War I? How did they keep up their strength and courage in the face of such carnage?

Below: A map showing the general location of the Western Front (line in red). This stable system of trenches appeared by December 1914 because of modern weapons such as artillery and machine guns, which made it difficult for troops to survive on the open battlefield.

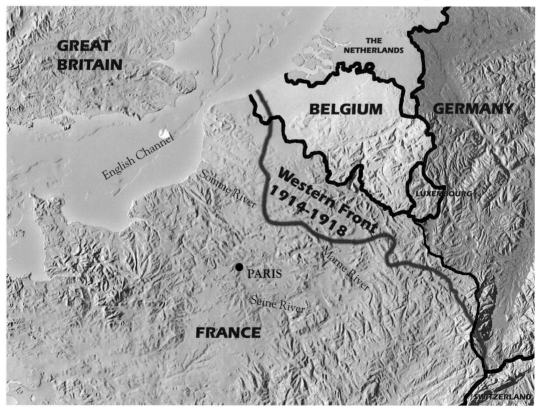

ANATOMY OF THE TRENCHES

Above: The Germans often constructed elaborate trenches, sometimes with electricity and wood paneling.
Facing page: A stone-built trench near Vimy, France.

THE TRENCHES OF THE WESTERN FRONT were more complicated than a single line of opposing ditches. Each side dug an elaborate system of forward trenches, supply trenches, communication trenches, and observation posts. Most of these trenches were interconnected, with men and supplies constantly moving back and forth between them.

The distance between the opposing trenches varied a great deal, but on average was approximately 755 feet (230 m), or about the length of 2.5 American football fields. They could be much farther apart, such as at Cambrai, where the trenches were 1,509 feet (460 m) apart. Sometimes they were much closer. The closest recorded distance between German and British troops was a section of trenches at Zonnebeke, Belgium, which was less than 23 feet (7 m), literally a stone's throw away.

A dead zone called no-man's-land separated the Allied and German trenches. Here, constant artillery barrages shattered the ground. It was a desolate landscape, filled with muddy craters, broken and blackened trees, tangles of barbed wire, the shells of bombed-out buildings, and the occasional wreck of a downed airplane.

IN THEIR OWN WORDS

"At 600 feet, we were free of most earthly noises and again I looked down. For the first time I saw the front line as it really was, mile upon mile of it. Now running straight, now turning this way or that in an apparently haphazard and unnecessary curve. The depth and complexity of the German trench system surprised me. No-man's-land, much wider in places than I had realized from any map, looked like a long-neglected racecourse by reason of the distinctive greenness of its bare but relatively undisturbed turf. Far behind, in enemy territory I saw factories with smoking chimneys and pleasantly normal villages."
—Aviator Billy Bishop

Above: Layers of barbed wire above this trench protect French soldiers in case of an enemy infantry attack. *Below right:* An American war photographer sets up a camera in a waterlogged trench on the Western Front.

The front line trenches were closest to the enemy. They were usually about 7 feet (2.1 m) deep and perhaps 6 feet (1.8 m) wide, but this varied a great deal, depending on the terrain and the particular army digging the trench. Most trenches weren't straight lines, but were dug in an irregular pattern. Seen from the air, British and German trenches looked like the battlements of a castle. If enemy troops ever fought their way into the trench, the pattern prevented them from simply shooting everyone down the entire line. The straight sections of forward trenches where the troops did their shooting were called firebays. Each was approximately 30 feet (9 m) long. The French preferred a simpler zigzag line. It was easier to build, but didn't offer as much protection.

Many of the trenches, especially Allied trenches in the lowlands of Belgium, were waterlogged. Mud was a constant hazard, and there was always a chance that the trench walls would collapse on the men. Wooden slats, called duckboards, were often placed on the trench floor to help soldiers walk. Sandbags lined both sides of the top of the trench, which gave it extra height and helped absorb the impact of bullets and artillery bursts. In front of the trench were rows of razor-sharp barbed wire to fend off enemy attacks.

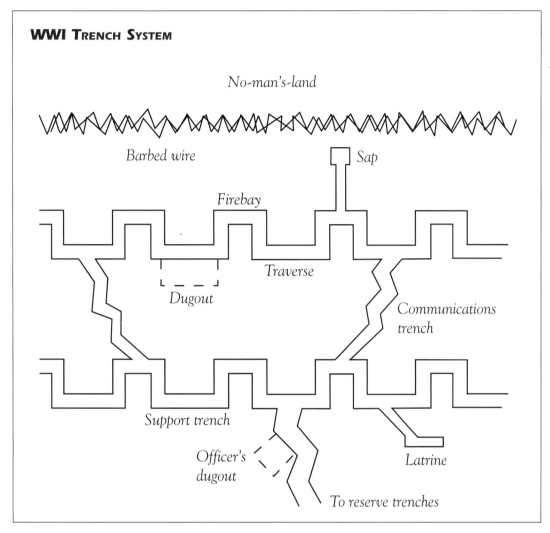

WWI Trench System

No-man's-land

Barbed wire

Sap

Firebay

Traverse

Dugout

Communications trench

Support trench

Officer's dugout

Latrine

To reserve trenches

A raised ledge, called a fire-step, was built or cut into the wall of the trench, about three feet (one m) from the floor. The men stood on the fire-step to see and shoot over the top. When the soldiers were ordered to "stand to," they stood on the fire-step awaiting an attack.

Saps were short trenches dug from the front line that projected out toward the enemy. They were narrow passages that ran 60 to 90 feet (18 to 27 m) forward, with just enough room at the end for two or three men. Some saps were simply large shell craters connected to the main line by a narrow trench. Saps were used as listening posts, especially at night. Sentries squatted in the darkness, waiting to raise the alarm at the slightest movement of the enemy.

Dugouts were underground shelters that gave the soldiers some protection against the weather and enemy artillery. The Allied generals didn't intend on staying in the trenches for long. They discouraged the men from building comfortable shelters. The Germans, however, considered the trench lines to be their new national borders, and built their elaborate trenches to last. Officers on both sides sometimes used dugouts that were reinforced with timbers or iron girders. Some dugouts, especially German dugouts farther back in the support trenches, had electricity, wood paneling, and even carpeting. In the front line trenches, however, the average soldier had to make do with a small hole burrowed out of the side of the trench wall. These personal "funk holes" were usually wet and infested with bugs and rodents. There was always the danger of the trench wall caving in, especially during heavy artillery shelling.

Below: A wounded soldier waits to be taken to a field hospital. Other troops sit in their personal "funk holes," which give some protection against enemy fire and the weather.

In the rear of the battlefield were miles of support and reserve trenches. Some German sections had as many as 10 lines of parallel trenches, all supporting each other. Men moved through these like insects in a hive, shuttling supplies and ammunition and providing reinforcements to soldiers manning the front line trenches. Connecting the support and reserve trenches with the front line was a system of communication trenches, which were also used to evacuate the wounded. Communication trenches were about the same size and depth as front line trenches. They didn't have firebays, but were built in a zigzag shape. Some communication trenches ran as long as three miles (five km).

Above: Soldiers walk through support trenches to carry supplies to front line troops.

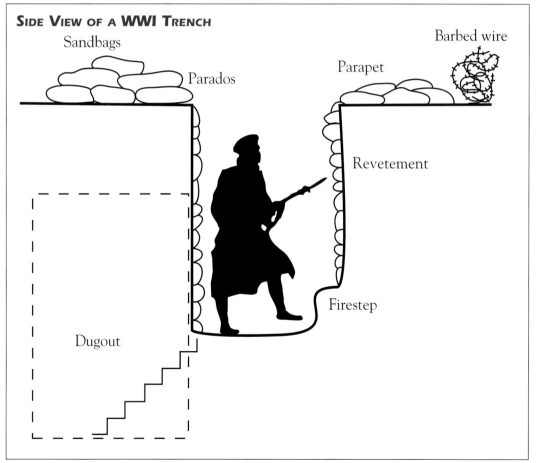

SIDE VIEW OF A WWI TRENCH

Sandbags

Parados

Barbed wire

Parapet

Revetement

Firestep

Dugout

Above: British troops perform their duties in an overcrowded trench.
Far right: A British soldier eats his dinner during a break in the fighting.

LIFE IN THE TRENCHES

A SOLDIER'S LIFE in the trenches of World War I was usually filled with two emotions, terror and boredom. Most military units spent several days on the front line, then a longer period in the reserve trenches farther back, followed by a few days of rest in neighboring towns or camps. A British division of 10,000 men might have only 1,000 soldiers stationed in the front line trenches at any one time. Attacks and offenses were also relatively rare. Sometimes soldiers never saw the enemy during their entire tour of duty.

The men were burdened with heavy packs. The average British private's equipment weighed 60 to 77 pounds (27 to 35 kg). Equipment included water, food, ammunition, a shovel, a gas mask, a coat, spare boots, wire-clippers for cutting through barbed wire, hand grenades, and personal belongings. Leather boots weighed five pounds (two kg) each. They often didn't fit correctly, which caused the soldiers great agony with every step. Steel helmets weighed about two pounds (one kg), depending on the army.

IN THEIR OWN WORDS

"We made straight for the trenches, but we've had vile weather, and I've been wet through for four days and nights. I lost all my socks and things before I left England, and hadn't the chance to make it up again, so I've been in trouble, particularly with bad heels; you can't have the slightest conception of what such an apparently trivial thing means. We've had shells bursting two yards off, bullets whizzing all over the show, but all you are aware of is the agony of your heels."
—Issac Rosenberg

When attacks came, usually at dawn or dusk, the action was intense, often accompanied by appalling slaughter. Death came in three main forms: artillery, machine guns, and rifle fire by snipers. The men hated rifle fire almost as much as artillery shelling. At least with artillery, they could hear it coming and take cover. But with rifle fire, once they heard the bullet go past—usually with a crack—it had already missed.

Robert Graves, the famous World War I author and poet, said that rifle fire gave the men a more immediate sense of danger. Bullets often first struck the barbed wire in front of the trenches, making the wire sing and dance, before they went zinging into the shattered woods behind the trenches. Most men didn't dare poke their heads above the lip of the trench for fear of getting shot by a sniper. Even a brief glance could prove fatal.

Above: An American soldier writes a letter home from the shelter of a dugout.

Artillery shelling often preceded an attack, and could sometimes last for days. The troops learned to tell what type of artillery shells were coming, and from where, by the sounds they made. Sometimes the shelling was so heavy that the noise became a presence all its own. It was a constant earth-shattering roar. The trenches gave decent protection from artillery shelling, except when a direct hit was scored. Many casualties of the war included men who simply vanished, blown apart by artillery or buried under trench cave-ins.

Above: Protected by gas masks, a machine gun crew fires at the enemy. *Right:* Soldiers go "over the top" in a frontal assault.

One special horror that all the men feared was poison gas. The first protective devices were very crude, nothing more than chemical-soaked pads to neutralize the gas. Sometimes the soldiers soaked gauze padding with their own urine, which actually worked to counteract the gas. By the end of the war, troops were issued protective masks with goggles and respirators.

Above: Allied troops await a German attack.

Some men couldn't handle the stress of trench warfare and committed suicide. Many more suffered psychological trauma. Shell shock, emotional exhaustion caused by the horrible conditions on the front, wasn't recognized as a real medical condition at the time. Sometimes the men suffered from their mental illness the rest of their lives.

Unprepared for the carnage they would be thrust into, a soldier's first trip to the front line trenches was often a shocking experience. Victor Silvester, a British infantryman, wrote in his diary, "We went up into the front-line near Arras, through sodden and devastated countryside. As we were moving up to our sector along the communication trenches, a shell burst ahead of me and one of my platoon dropped. He was the first man I ever saw killed. Both his legs were blown off and the whole of his face and body was peppered with shrapnel. The sight turned my stomach. I was sick and terrified, but even more frightened of showing it.

"That night I had been asleep in a dugout about three hours when I woke up feeling something biting my hip. I put my hand down and my fingers closed on a big rat. It had nibbled through my haversack, my tunic and pleated kilt to get at my flesh. With a cry of horror I threw it from me."

When the enemy wasn't trying to kill the soldiers, nature tried its best to finish the job. Crude sanitary conditions caused disease. Soldiers were forced to endure the filth from unwashed men, urine and excrement, food waste, swarms of flies, lice, legions of field mice, frogs, and even half-buried corpses.

Rats seemed to be everywhere in the trenches. They spread disease, and constantly harassed the men. The brown variety were especially vicious. Many men suffered bites. The rats reproduced by the millions, and kept themselves fat by feeding on the half-buried bodies of the soldiers.

Burying corpses was always a problem. Leonard Thompson, a British soldier, wrote in his journal, "We set to work to bury people. We pushed them into the sides of the trenches but bits of them kept getting uncovered and sticking out, like people in a badly made bed. Hands were the worst; they would escape from the sand, pointing, begging—even waving! There was one which we all shook when we passed, saying 'Good morning,' in a posh voice. Everybody did it. The bottom of the trench was springy like a mattress because of all the bodies underneath."

Above: German soldiers show off a catch of trench rats.

Lice were another common hazard. They got into the men's uniforms, and were very difficult to get rid of. The men sometimes used candles or matches to burn the lice from the seams of their clothes, but it was a tricky operation to kill the lice and keep the clothing from catching on fire. Lice eggs hatched as soon as they got warm from body heat. The pests bit the flesh and caused horrible itching. Lice also carried a disease called pyrexia, which was known as trench fever.

Rain made conditions even more miserable in the trenches, especially for the British, who occupied the northern, lowland areas. The bottoms of the trenches filled with mud, sometimes knee-deep. Shell holes usually filled up with water, creating a muddy quagmire. Men going on the attack in no-man's-land often fell into these holes, sometimes drowning in the mud. It was a much feared way to die.

Because the men went a long time without changing their wet boots and socks, many developed a condition called trench foot. Similar to frostbite in its symptoms, trench foot caused the feet to go numb, and then turn red or blue. In very bad cases, gangrene set in, which meant that the tissue had died. In that case, toes, or even the whole foot, had to be amputated. Over the course of the war, nearly 75,000 British troops were hospitalized in France from trench foot.

Above: German troops pass the time during a lull in the fighting.

IN THEIR OWN WORDS

Gas! GAS! Quick, boys!—An ecstasy of fumbling
Fitting the clumsy helmets just in time,
But someone still was yelling out and stumbling
And flound'ring like a man in fire or lime.—
Dim through the misty panes and thick green light,
As under a green sea, I saw him drowning.
—Wilfred Owen
Excerpt from *Dulce et decorum est*

NIGHT PATROL

ONE OF THE DUTIES OF OFFICERS was to go on night patrol into no-man's-land to collect information on the enemy. Officers took a small number of men with them,

usually no more than one or two. German night patrols tended to be larger, sometimes six or seven men, and many without an officer present. Soldiers on night patrol crept through no-man's-land, wriggling past fields of barbed wire and into muddy shell holes, trying to get within earshot of the enemy. It was a nerve-racking experience; the slightest sound or movement could bring quick death from the enemy.

Above: German soldiers cut a path through barbed wire before venturing into no-man's-land.
Far right: Soldiers scramble for safety during an artillery bombardment.

IN THEIR OWN WORDS

From the diary of Second Lieutenant H.E. Cooper
115th Battalion, Royal Warwickshire Regiment

"Let me try to picture what it is like. I am asked to take out an 'officer's patrol' of seven men; duties—get out to the position of the German listening post (we know it), wait for their patrol and 'scupper' it; also discover what work is being done in their trenches . . .

"As soon as the dusk is sufficiently dark, we get out into the front of the trenches by climbing up on to the parapet and tumbling over as rapidly as possible so as not to be silhouetted against the last traces of the sunset. No man feels afraid for we have grown accustomed to this thing now, but every man knows that he has probably seen his last sunset, for this is the most dangerous thing in war. Out we walk through the barbed wire entanglement zone through which an approaching enemy must climb, but we have a zigzag path through the thirty yards or so of prickly unpleasantness. . . .

"We lie down in the long grass and listen. . . . I arrange my men in pairs—one to go in front and one to either flank, the corporal and myself remaining in rear, but the whole party is quite close together, practically within whispering distance of one another. We all advance slowly and carefully, wriggling along through the long grass for a hundred yards or so. . . . There we lie and wait and listen. One pair goes out another fifty yards or so, nearly to the German wire to see if there is anything about. Nothing is discernible, so they return, and for another hour we lie in absolute silence like spiders waiting for flies. It is a weary game and extremely trying to one's nerves, for every sense especially hearing and sight are strained to the utmost. . . . Nothing is to be heard near us, but there is a very ominous sign—no shots are being fired from the trenches in front of us, no flares are being sent up and there is no working party out. This points to only one thing and that is that they also have a patrol out. There is no other conclusion.

Below: A French and American raiding party picks its way through the shattered ruins of no-man's-land.

"Suddenly quite close to the corporal and myself there is a heavy rustling in the long grass on the right. Now, if never before, I know the meaning of—is it fear? My heart thumps so heavily that they surely must hear it, my face is covered with a cold perspiration, my revolver hammer goes back with a sharp click and my hand trembles. I have no inclination to run away—quite the reverse—but I have one solitary thought: I am going to kill a man. This I repeat over and over again, and the thought makes me miserable and at the same time joyful for I shall have accounted for one of the blackguards even if I go myself. Do they know we are here? How many are there? Are they armed with bombs like most German patrols? However, our queries remain unanswered, for quite abruptly they change their direction and make off to the right where to follow them would be only courting certain disaster.

"So with great caution we come in and breathe again when we are safely inside the trench. I give instructions to the sentries to fire low down into the grass but it is very improbable that the German patrol will get anything but a fright."

Above: A German machine gun crew listens for the sound of an enemy raiding party.

OVER THE TOP

THOUGH ARTILLERY caused thousands of deaths in World War I, the most likely way to be killed was by scrambling up and out of the trenches in a frontal attack, right into the path of enemy machine gun fire. Year after year, millions of men were ordered to go "over the top," which caused horrific numbers of casualties. Disastrous full frontal assaults resulted in whole companies of men getting mowed down. Still, the generals ordered more attacks.

The soldiers continued to do their duty, not out of blind obedience, but more out of fear of letting their comrades down. Each man was intensely afraid of death or injury, but struggled not to show it. Most would rather be dead than be proven cowards.

Once the dawn whistle blew, signaling the attack, and the men dashed forward, fear melted away, to be replaced by movement, noise, the smell of gunpowder, and utter confusion. The lack of fear once the fight began was a common experience. A British infantryman who survived the Battle of Loos wrote, "The moment had come when it was unwise to think…. To dwell for a moment on the novel position of being standing where a thousand deaths swept by, missing you by a mere hair's breadth would be sheer folly."

Below: Canadian troops rush out of the trenches and into combat.

Thomas Hudson, a British private in the Lancashire Fusiliers, wrote in his diary, "It is utterly impossible to describe one's feelings during the hours of waiting for 'zero hour'—the mind is full of wild thoughts and fancies etc which are utterly beyond control. Recollections of friends and dear ones, places we have seen and known and different phases of life all seem to pass in review before one's eyes and one is recalled to the bitter realities of the moment by the officer's voice: 'Fifteen minutes to go, boys, get ready.' Immediately there is a great stir and excitement, a final setting of equipment etc and examination of arms and then a handshake with one or two dear comrades. 6:45 a.m., 'Over you go, boys,' and we are away on that strange journey across 'No-Man's Land.'"

Until the spring of 1918, assaults on both sides resulted in minimal capturing of enemy territory. Even when sections of enemy trenches were taken, counterassaults usually regained any lost ground within days. The only thing to show for the effort was more casualties. As the dead and wounded piled up year after year, many soldiers became convinced that the war would never have an end.

Above: Despite German shells bursting overhead, an Allied officer leads his men out of the trenches during the Arras and Cambrai offensive on April 7, 1918.

THE DEAD REMEMBERED

OF ALL THE ALLIED CASUALTIES on the Western Front in World War I, about one third were caused by the horrible conditions in the trenches. However, while 31 percent of battle casualties eventually died of their wounds, less than one percent died from sickness. Still, even when a soldier survived the war, the horrors of the trenches would haunt him the rest of his life.

Below: A dead soldier lies next to his machine gun.

Many well-known writers and poets produced work based on their experiences in World War I. It was an era when the arts were heavily censored during war years. American author Ernest Hemingway wrote in *Men at War*, "…there was no really good true war book during the entire four years of war. The only true writing that came through during the war was in poetry. One reason for this is that poets are not arrested as quickly as prose writers…."

British poets were well recognized, especially for their anti-war writings. They included Siegfried Sassoon, Edmund Thomas, Wilfred Owen, and Rupert Brook.

Perhaps the best-known poem of World War I was "In Flanders Fields" by Canadian poet John McCrae. He was a physician who fought on the Western Front in 1914. McCrae wrote the sonnet after witnessing millions of bright red poppies blooming on the battlefields of northern France and Belgium where his friends lay buried. "In Flanders Fields" symbolized the sacrifices of the millions of men who fought and died in World War I.

"In Flanders Fields" by John McCrae

In Flanders fields the poppies blow
Between the crosses, row on row
That mark our place; and in the sky
The larks, still bravely singing, fly
Scarce heard amid the guns below.

We are the Dead. Short days ago
We lived, felt dawn, saw sunset glow,
Loved and were loved, and now we lie
In Flanders fields.

Take up our quarrel with the foe:
To you from failing hands we throw
The torch; be yours to hold it high.
If ye break faith with us who die
We shall not sleep, though poppies grow
In Flanders fields.

TIMELINE

1906 *February:* HMS *Dreadnought* is launched by Great Britain, beginning a worldwide naval arms race.

1914 *June 28:* Austria-Hungary's Archduke Franz Ferdinand is assassinated by a Serbian nationalist while touring Sarajevo, the capital of Bosnia-Herzegovina.

1914 *August:* World War I begins as German armed forces invade Belgium and France. Most of Europe, including Great Britain and Russia, soon enters the war.

1914 *August 26-31:* Russia suffers a major defeat at the Battle of Tannenberg.

1914 *September 9-14:* Second massive Russian defeat, this time at the Battle of the Masurian Lakes.

1915 Turkish forces slaughter ethnic Armenians living within the Ottoman Empire. The Turkish government accuses the Armenians of helping the Russians. Casualty totals vary widely, with estimates between 800,000 and 2 million Armenians killed.

1915 *Spring:* German Zeppelins launch bombing raids over English cities.

1915 *April 22:* Germans are first to use lethal poison gas on a large scale during the Battle of Ypres.

1915 *May 7:* A German U-boat sinks the unarmed British passenger liner *Lusitania*, killing 1,198 people, including 128 Americans. The American public is outraged, but President Wilson manages to keep the U.S. neutral.

1916 *February 21-December 18:* The Battle of Verdun. Nearly one million soldiers are killed or wounded.

1916 *June 24-November 13:* The Battle of the Somme costs approximately 1.25 million casualties. On the first day of the infantry attack, July 1, British forces suffered a staggering 60,000 casualties, including 20,000 dead, the largest single-day casualty total in British military history. Many troops are killed by a new battlefield weapon, the machine gun.

1917 *January 31:* Germany declares unrestricted submarine warfare, outraging the American public.

1917 *March 12:* The Russian Revolution overthrows Tsar Nicholas II.

1917 *April 6:* The United States declares war on Germany.

1917 *November:* Tanks are used for the first time on a large scale at the Battle of Cambrai. And on November 7, Russia is taken over by Lenin's communist government during the Bolshevik Revolution.

1917 *December 15:* Russia's Bolshevik government agrees to a separate peace with Germany, taking Russia out of the war.

1918 *March 21-July 19:* Germany mounts five "Ludendorff offensives" against strengthening Allied forces. The attacks are costly to both sides, but Germany fails to crush the Allied armies.

1918 *May 30-June 17:* American forces are successful against the Germans at Chateau-Thierry and Belleau Woods.

1918 *September 26-November 11:* French and American forces launch the successful Meuse-Argonne Offensive.

1918 *September 27-October 17:* British forces break through the Hindenburg Line in several places.

1918 *November 11:* Armistice Day. Fighting stops at 11:00 A.M.

1919 *May 7-June 28:* The Treaty of Versailles is written and signed.

GLOSSARY

ARTILLERY

Large guns, too heavy to carry, that fire explosive shells at the enemy from a great distance. Coordinated artillery barrages can cause massive destruction without exposing friendly ground troops to enemy fire.

AUTOMATIC WEAPON

A type of firearm that uses the force of the explosion of a shell to eject the empty cartridge case, put the next shell in position, and then fire it. This sequence continues as long as the trigger is pressed. A machine gun is an example of an automatic weapon.

CASUALTY

Soldiers killed or wounded in battle.

CREEPING BARRAGE

Also called a rolling barrage. Just before the infantry charged enemy trench lines, artillery sometimes laid down a creeping barrage, a steady curtain of bombs that slowly moved forward. In theory, the creeping barrage would clear the way for advancing infantry troops. In practice, however, the barrages could be poorly timed and inaccurate. Extended artillery fire often did nothing more than alert the enemy to an impending infantry charge across no-man's-land.

FIREBAY

The forward part of a front line trench where soldiers shoot at the enemy.

FIRE-STEP

A raised platform built into the wall of a trench so that soldiers can raise their weapons over the lip of the trench and fire at the enemy.

HOWITZER

A short cannon that delivers its explosive shell in a high arc. Howitzers are useful for lobbing bombs when the enemy is relatively close, such as in an opposing trench position.

NO-MAN'S-LAND
The area of land between two opposing lines of trenches.

OVER THE TOP
When one side advances out of the shelter of the trenches into no-man's-land and attacks the enemy.

SAP
A section of trench running at a right angle to a front line trench, which projects toward the enemy for several yards. Saps were used as listening posts to detect enemy attacks. Sometimes these listening posts were simply large shell craters connected to the front line trench by a narrow passage.

SNIPER
A soldier who fires at the enemy from a hidden position, sometimes from a great distance. During World War I, sniper fire often struck men as they exposed their heads and upper torsos to peer over the lip of the trenches.

TRENCH FOOT
A common ailment suffered by many soldiers in the trenches of World War I. Trench foot was caused by the wet and muddy conditions, and a lack of dry socks and boots. In severe cases, diseased toes or feet had to be amputated.

WESTERN FRONT
Established by December 1914, the Western Front was a network of trenches that stretched across eastern France and a section of western Belgium. The Western Front ran approximately 400 miles (645 km), reaching from the North Sea to the border of Switzerland.

WEB SITES

Would you like to learn more about the trenches of World War I? Please visit **www.abdopub.com** to find up-to-date Web site links. These links are routinely monitored and updated to provide the most current information available.

INDEX

Left: Soldiers take cover in a sheltered dugout on the Western Front.